Cornerstones of Freedom

The Spirit of St. Louis

R. Conrad Stein

CHILDRENS PRESS®

CHICAGO

Library of Congress Cataloging-in-Publication Data

Stein, R. Conrad.
  The Spirit of St. Louis / by R. Conrad Stein.
    p. cm. – (Cornerstones of freedom)
  ISBN 0-516-06682-X
  1. Lindbergh, Charles A. (Charles Augustus), 1902–1974 –
Juvenile literature. 2. Spirit of St. Louis (Airplane) – Juvenile
literature. 3. Transatlantic flights – Juvenile literature.
4. Air pilots – United States – Biography – Juvenile literature.
[1. Lindbergh, Charles A. (Charles Augustus), 1902–1974.
2. Spirit of St. Louis (Airplane) 3. Transatlantic flights.
4. Air pilots.] I. Title. II. Series.
TL540.L5S728 1994
629.13'092 – dc20   94-9491
                                                        CIP
                                                        AC

Paris, France. May 8, 1927. 5:00 A.M.

At Le Bourget Airfield, an excited crowd gathered hoping to witness history. Two French aviators were about to climb into the sky and try to fly nonstop to New York. Piloting the airplane called the *White Bird* was a World War I ace named Charles Nungesser. Another experienced airman named Francois Coli served as navigator.

The crowd fell silent as the buzz of the single engine became a roar. The plane bumped slowly along the runway. Sitting in the open cockpit, pilot Nungesser shouted to the crowd. His words were drowned out by the screaming engine, but

Coli (left) and Nungesser prepare for takeoff.

the spectators could read his lips: *"Au revoir. Au revoir."* ("Good-bye. Good-bye.") Loaded down with almost nine hundred gallons of gasoline, the plane stubbornly resisted takeoff. Nungesser kept the throttle at full speed, rolling the aircraft faster, faster, faster. Finally, after speeding across almost a mile of runway, the wheels left the ground.

At first, the flight progressed exactly according to schedule. An hour and a half after takeoff, the *White Bird* was seen crossing the English Channel. Five hours later, it was spotted near the coast of Ireland.

Then hours passed. Too many hours crept by, and the plane had not been seen over North America. The next day, the United States Navy began a massive search, but neither the bodies of the aviators nor the wreckage of their plane

Preparations are made to search for the missing French airmen.

was found. The *White Bird* had crashed in either the freezing waters of the Atlantic or the wilds of Newfoundland. Two more men had died trying to fly between New York and Paris.

In 1919, a New York hotel owner named Raymond Orteig had offered a $25,000 prize to the first pilot or crew to fly nonstop between the two cities. Nungesser and Coli were the fifth and sixth airmen to lose their lives attempting the flight.

While the world mourned the loss of the two Frenchmen, an American pilot readied his airplane to attempt the Paris flight. He was a quiet, shy, twenty-five-year-old bachelor named Charles Augustus Lindbergh. Unlike other pilots competing for the prize money, Lindbergh was not a famous aviator. But he was tough, intelligent, and perhaps the best pilot in America.

Aviation was just a quarter of a century old at

December 17, 1903: The Wright brothers make their historic first flight.

the time Lindbergh and others attempted the jump between continents. In 1903, Orville and Wilbur Wright had launched a new era when their flying machine struggled into the air at a hill near Kitty Hawk, North Carolina.

Soon after the Wright brothers' flight, other flying machines appeared. Those early aircraft were little more than motorized kites. They were built on frames made of sticks, held together with baling wire, covered with muslin cloth, and driven by engines about as powerful as those on today's lawn mowers.

Still, these fragile machines took up the challenge of conquering distance. Flying became

Aviators of the early 1900s tried a number of extraordinary ideas to get their flying machines airborne.

a contest pitting humans against natural barriers. In 1909, a Frenchman named Louis Blériot became the first man to fly across the English Channel. Crossing the twenty-three-mile channel took the French pilot thirty-six minutes. In 1911, Calbraith Perry Rodgers completed the first solo flight across the United States in his plane, the *Vin Fiz.* In 1913, France's Roland Garros was the first to cross the Mediterranean Sea.

Blériot in flight

World War I (1914–1918) put an end to the marathon distance flights. But during the war, aircraft design improved tremendously. When peace came, aviators dreamed of overcoming the greatest of all natural barriers—the Atlantic Ocean.

In the skies above the Atlantic, pilots had to fly into the teeth of gales that could slow their aircraft almost to a walk. They had to push through clouds of freezing mist that coated their planes' wings with ice. Finally, the immense size of the ocean staggered the minds of pilots. Even at its shortest point, between Newfoundland and Ireland, the Atlantic Ocean stretched some 1,900 miles.

In June 1919, two British airmen named John Alcock and Arthur Whitten-Brown climbed aboard a fragile-looking double-engined biplane.

They took off from a cow pasture in Newfound-land and headed out to sea. Sixteen hours later, they crash-landed in a marsh on the coast of Ireland. Their voyage had been perilous, but their achievement incredible. Midway across the Atlantic, they almost plunged into the water while lost in an ice cloud. Near the Irish coast, one of their engines began sputtering, and they were running dangerously low on fuel. Yet history records the Englishmen Alcock and Whitten-Brown as the first to fly nonstop across the Atlantic Ocean.

Alcock and Whitten-Brown's triumphant flight ended with a hard landing in Ireland.

Aviators still dreamed of doing more than merely crossing the Atlantic at its narrowest stretch. The ability to travel nonstop between major cities on both continents represented a whole new age of transportation. When Raymond Orteig offered his $25,000 prize, the New York-to-Paris flight became an obsession among airmen of the 1920s.

May 20, 1927, was a misty morning at Roosevelt Field, New York. Before climbing aboard, Charles Lindbergh posed for pictures in front of his plane, the *Spirit of St. Louis*. Because St. Louis businessmen had helped him to buy his plane, Lindbergh named the craft *Spirit of St. Louis*. Unlike the previous planes to attempt the flight, Lindbergh's had a single seat. To save weight, Lindbergh had decided to fly solo.

Charles Lindbergh poses before climbing aboard the Spirit of St. Louis.

From the takeoff to landing, Lindbergh's voyage would span 3,600 miles. For a 1927 aircraft, that was an unthinkable distance for a nonstop flight. The *Spirit of St. Louis* was loaded down with more than 400 gallons of gasoline, pushing the plane's total weight over 5,000 pounds. This was more than the wings were designed to carry. Complicating matters, rain had fallen the night before and the aircraft wheels had sunk to their axles in mud.

As the crowd waits anxiously, Lindbergh makes his final preparations.

A crowd gathered in the early morning haze to cheer the takeoff. The weather conditions were terrible and forecasts were even worse. But at exactly 7:52 A.M., Charles Lindbergh started his

Lindbergh in the first moments of his historic flight

engine and began rolling his airplane slowly forward. "The *Spirit of St. Louis* feels more like a truck than an airplane," Lindbergh later wrote.

At the end of the muddy runway stood a line of telephone poles with wires strung between them. As the engine roared, the plane bumped up to the speed of 30, then 40 miles per hour. The telephone lines suddenly loomed dangerously close. There was not enough runway left to stop even if Lindbergh had chosen to. The straining engine seemed to be shaking the aircraft to pieces. Water and mud splattered against the bottoms of the wings. Finally, Lindbergh felt the plane's weight shift from wheels to wings. He made it into the air, just barely clearing the telephone lines.

Lindbergh eased his aircraft into a cruising altitude. Then he slouched in his seat and thought of the many hours and miles that lay ahead of him. His only provisions consisted of five sandwiches and a quart of water. Regarding food, Lindbergh had told a member of his ground crew, "If I get to Paris, I won't need any more. And if I don't get there, I won't need any more either."

Charles Augustus Lindbergh was born on February 4, 1902, in Detroit, Michigan. He spent most of his childhood on a farm in Minnesota. His father was a lawyer who later became a United States congressman.

Young Charles Lindbergh and his dog

His mother taught high school chemistry. Despite having gifted parents, Lindbergh was a poor student. He did show flashes of brilliance in math and had a marvelous mechanical ability. He was able to fix any kind of motor regardless of its condition.

When he was a boy on his parents' farm, Charles heard a buzzing in the sky and looked up to see an airplane soaring through the clouds.

13

Barnstormers performed all sorts of wild and daring stunts while in flight. A common routine involved wing walking (right), in which one or more daredevils would boldly walk along the wing of a flying plane. Charles Lindbergh tried wing walking several times and later said it wasn't quite as dangerous as it looked to people on the ground.

This photo shows air mail pilot Lindbergh seated in the plane as the mail is loaded aboard.

A chilling feeling swept over him. He knew his destiny would be in the skies. For the rest of his life, aviation became like a religion to him. He later wrote that long, lonely flights enabled him to commune with ghosts and guardian spirits.

Lindbergh attended the University of Wisconsin for two years but dropped out to enroll in a flight school. There, the once poor student finished first in his class. Upon receiving his pilot's license, Lindbergh took up barnstorming. Barnstormers were daredevil pilots who performed dangerous aerial stunts at carnivals and fairs.

After barnstorming for two years, Lindbergh became a flier for the United States Air Mail Service. Flying the mail in the 1920s was a job for skilled aviators only. Lindbergh and others

Lindbergh as an air mail pilot

15

had to fly great distances in nasty weather. During those long flights, Lindbergh's ears were attuned to even the smallest change in the purr of the motor. "Let a cylinder miss once," he wrote, "and I'll feel it as clearly as though a human heart had skipped against my thumb."

Lindbergh was also a gifted writer. Twenty-five years after his Paris flight, he wrote a book called *The Spirit of St. Louis*. It gave a thrilling hour-by-hour account of his lonely flight over the mighty Atlantic. He wrote the book largely in present tense, so it reads like an event happening at the moment.

Lindberg wrote about how he felt when he crossed the New York shoreline: "I'm alone at last, over the first short stretch of sea on the route to France. It's only 35 miles to the Connecticut shore, but I've never flown across that much water before."

Flying over water was Lindbergh's only weakness as a pilot. The midwesterner had never before ventured near an ocean in his plane. But he knew the dangers of ice clouds—massive gray pillows in the air that seemed to prowl the Atlantic like beasts on the hunt. In his book he described ice clouds with a feeling of terror only a pilot could express: "They enmesh intruders. They're barbaric in their methods. They toss you in their inner turbulence, lash you with their hailstones, poison you with freezing mist."

Lindbergh's flight was only an hour old, but the immensity of the ocean suddenly overwhelmed him. He already began to doubt his chances. "Looking ahead at the unbroken horizon and limitless expanse of water, I'm struck by my arrogance in attempting such a flight. I'm giving up a continent and heading out to sea in the most fragile vehicle ever designed by man. . . . Why have I dared stake my life on the belief . . . that I can find my way through shifting air to Europe?"

But the ocean gradually looked less forbidding. He dropped down until his wheels were skimming just six feet above the water's surface. "The *Spirit of St. Louis* is like a butterfly blown out to sea. How often I used to watch [butterflies], as a child, on the banks of the Mississippi,

This photo was one of the last taken of the Spirit of St. Louis *as it passed over North America and headed out to the Atlantic.*

17

Preparing for a practice flight, Lindbergh straps on a parachute. He embarked on his flight across the Atlantic without a parachute because he did not want to carry the extra weight.

dancing up and down above the water, as I am doing now. . . . But a touch of wing to water, and they were down forever, just as my plane would be. Why, I used to wonder, did [the butterflies] ever leave the safety of land? But why have I? How similar my position has become."

Soaring above the waves, the *Spirit of St. Louis* looked like a delicate silver toy. Lindbergh had helped to design the plane. It was 28 feet long with a wingspan of 46 feet. This made it a small aircraft even by 1927 standards. It was powered by a newly designed engine that had nine cylinders jutting out of a single crankcase like the spokes of a wheel. The lightweight engine was unusually powerful. To save weight, Lindbergh had refused to carry a radio, and had even refused to take a parachute. Yet the *Spirit of St. Louis* was so loaded with fuel that the motor could manage an air speed of only 102 miles per hour.

During his fourth hour aloft, Lindbergh remembered that he hadn't gotten any sleep in his last night on the ground. "It would be pleasant to doze off a few seconds. But I mustn't feel sleepy at this stage of the trip! Why I'm less than a tenth of the way to Paris." He also noticed a clump of mud that had plastered itself onto the bottom of one of his wings during takeoff. "I wanted to reach out and scrape it off . . . but it's an arm's length too far away. Why should I have to carry its extra weight and resistance all the way across the ocean?" He knew a little clump of mud couldn't slow him down by more than a fraction of a mile per hour. But because he was so tired, his mind was wandering, and that clump of mud was aggravating him.

Lindbergh flew a northerly circular course designed to take him back over land once more before his final ocean crossing. The fifth hour found him flying over the wilds of Nova Scotia in Canada. The need for sleep still gripped him. He stuck a hand out the window and scooped cold air against his face to keep himself awake. Luckily, his engine still throbbed a steady beat.

He risked burning extra fuel to buzz over the town of St. John's, Newfoundland. Townspeople waved up at him. Then he banked his plane over the Atlantic, pointing the nose to the east. St. John's was Lindbergh's final reference point on North America. For the next 2,000 miles to

Ireland, his entire vista would be filled by water and ice floes. He would be flying blind, guided only by his compass, with no mapped land-masses below to mark his position.

Ships typically avoided the northerly route Lindbergh had chosen. He quickly understood why. Suddenly, shockingly, he realized he had entered the menacing realm of the Arctic. Below him sprawled a huge ice field that looked like a frozen desert. "As far as I can see ahead, the ocean is glaring white. . . . I feel surrounded by the stillness of [it]—the frozen silence of the north. I feel a trespasser in the forbidden latitudes, in air where such a little plane and I have no authority to be."

Night fell suddenly, as if a blanket had been pulled across the sky. Fog enveloped the airplane. The luminous dials of the instrument panel stared up at Lindbergh with ghostlike eyes. His life depended on the compass needle. If his compass failed, or if he erred in reading it, he might fly in endless circles above the Atlantic until he ran out of gas.

Lindbergh suddenly felt his plane's wings shudder. The *Spirit of St. Louis* shook as if caught in the fist of an angry giant. Lindbergh found his flashlight and shined the beam along a wing. *Ice!* Because of the fog, he had flown blindly into an ice cloud. These were the very dreaded monsters he had hoped to avoid.

"I've got to turn around, get back into clear air—quickly!" He knew that if he jerked his rudder, he could lose control of his aircraft in the wild currents. Telling himself to be calm, Lindbergh began a long, lazy turn. His eyes locked on the instrument panel. Already he had lost ten miles per hour in air speed and a hundred feet in altitude. This was caused by the crust of ice growing on the wings. The longer he remained in the clouds, the thicker the coating of ice would become. Still, Lindbergh continued his gradual turn. One fast move could mean a fatal plunge into the sea.

Then, finally, "My eyes sense a change in the blackness of my cockpit. I look out the window. Can these be the same stars? Is this the same

The interior of the Spirit of St. Louis —Lindbergh stared directly into the instrument panel and had to stretch his neck to see through a window.

sky? How bright! How clear! What safety I have reached!"

After waiting a few minutes, Lindbergh turned his flashlight on the wings once more. The ice was receding. But somehow that stubborn clump of mud remained cemented on his wing. He cursed it.

In the starlit night, Lindbergh discovered that he was surrounded by ice clouds. Their gray shapes rose out of the Atlantic like giant inverted icicles. "Great cliffs tower over me, ward me off with icy walls. They belong to mountains of another world. . . . To plunge into these mountains of the heavens would be like stepping into quicksand." He pressed on, weaving between the ice clouds much like a hiker in mountain country threads through valleys.

During his nineteenth hour in the air, Lindbergh reached the point of no return. He no longer had enough fuel to turn back to America. He would either land in Europe or crash into the sea. "I've burned my last bridge behind me."

Sleep. How delicious it would be to catch just five minutes of sleep. But Lindbergh knew that if he dozed off for even a few seconds, he would be likely to wake up in a spinning dive. He stamped his feet. He stretched his neck to put his face into the slipstream outside. He shouted in the cockpit at the top of his lungs. Anything to fight off dozing. But the steady drone of the

engine sounded like a dangerous lullaby. "I'm
passing out. . . . Can I hold onto consciousness?"

To the east, the sun inched over the horizon.
The pilot saw long fingers of red stretching into
the sky. He had survived the ordeal of a night
alone over the Atlantic.

Lindbergh flew as if he were in a trance.
Although no longer sleepy, he felt somehow
unreal. He thought he saw islands jutting out of
the blue water, but he knew land was still many
hours away. At one point, he believed he had
visitors in his tiny plane. "The fuselage behind
me becomes filled with ghostly presences. . . .
These phantoms speak with human voices,
conversing and advising me on my flight,
discussing problems of my navigation,
reassuring me."

His twenty-seventh hour aloft found Lindbergh dreamily buzzing over the waves when he saw a curious white speck in the water. Were his eyes still playing tricks? No, there was another one. Fishing boats! This meant that the coast of Ireland had to be near.

Lindbergh slowed his engine to a soft throb. His plane glided inches above one of the boats' sails.

He shouted down to the boat, "Hey, where's Ireland? Which way is Ireland?"

A shocked fisherman poked his head out of a porthole. He was so stunned he could only stare at the tiny airplane, neither waving nor uttering a word.

An hour or so later, Lindbergh spotted land. This time it was no hallucination. First he saw a few rocks in the mist. Then a coastline. Ireland! Roaring over the shoreline, Lindbergh became the first man to fly the Atlantic alone.

Wide awake now, Lindbergh soared over Ireland and the southern tip of England.

This map tracks Lindbergh's entire trip across the Atlantic. The inset map also shows his earlier flight from San Diego (where the Spirit of St. Louis was built and tested) to New York.

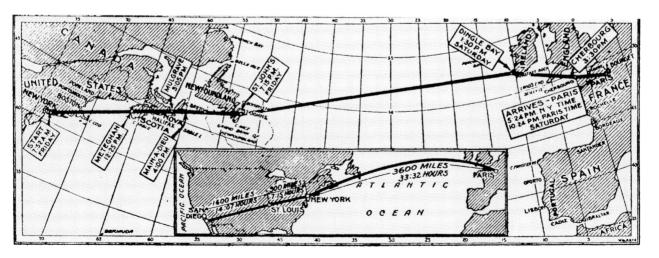

Below, people waved at his tiny silver plane. In turn, Lindbergh banked his wings. Unknown to Lindbergh, radios shouted the news to the entire world: "He did it. That crazy Yank did it. He made it across the Atlantic!"

Night fell again, but the skies were clear. Lindbergh saw streetlights and automobile lights burning below before he crossed the English Channel. Over France, he followed the River Seine. Ahead, a huge patch of light glowed like a distant fire—Paris. He had endured thirty-three hours in the air. Now, strangely, he regretted that it was all over. In the center of the brightly lighted avenues of Paris, Lindbergh spotted the Eiffel Tower. He circled it once, found Le Bourget Airfield, and landed. Then all of Paris found him.

Lindbergh arrived in Paris at night and saw the spectacular Eiffel Tower (below); after he landed at Le Bourget Airfield, the surging crowd nearly injured him and damaged his airplane.

Lindbergh became an instant hero around the world. American Ambassador Myron T. Merrick (below, left and right) led the cheers in Paris; Lindbergh then toured Europe in the Spirit of St. Louis *(right); meanwhile, back in Minnesota, locals prepared for a grand homecoming (bottom right).*

The New York Times.

**LINDBERGH DOES IT! TO PARIS IN 33½ HOURS;
FLIES 1,000 MILES THROUGH SNOW AND SLEET;
CHEERING FRENCH CARRY HIM OFF FIELD**

COULD HAVE GONE 500 MILES FARTHER

Gasoline for at Least That Much More
Flew at Times From 10 Feet to
10,000 Feet Above Water.

ATE ONLY ONE AND A HALF OF HIS FIVE SANDWICHES

Fell Asleep at Times but Quickly Awoke—Glimpses
of His Adventure in Brief Interview
at the Embassy.

CROWD ROARS THUNDEROUS WELCOME

Breaks Through Lines of Soldiers and
Police and Surging to Plane
Weary Flier from His Cockpit

AVIATORS RESCUE HIM FROM FRENZIED MOB

Paris Boulevards Ring With Celebration
and Night Watch—American Flag
Is Called For and Wildly Acclaimed

**LEVINE ABANDONS
BELLANCA FLIGHT**

**LINDBERGH TRIUMPH
THRILLS COOLIDGE**

**New York Stages Big Celebration
After Hours of Anxious Waiting**

A crowd of about 100,000 people poured onto the airfield to greet the American. People pulled Lindbergh out of his cockpit and passed him overhead hand to hand. Luckily, two French aviators rescued Lindbergh and hurried him to the hangar. Lindbergh was frightened by being nearly crushed, and he feared that the uncontrollable crowd would damage his plane.

The celebration continued overnight, and for weeks thereafter. Lindbergh came home to a New York ticker tape parade that has never been equaled. *The New York Times* devoted its first sixteen pages to stories about him and his flight.

He was called the "Lone Eagle" and "Lucky Lindy." He toured the nation with the *Spirit of St. Louis*. He was given the Congressional

Returning to American soil, Lindbergh received a ticker tape parade in New York (right) and was honored by President Calvin Coolidge in Washington, D.C. (left).

Soon after his triumphant flight, Lindbergh married Anne Morrow. Three years later, their baby son was kidnapped and murdered.

Medal of Honor in December. Charles Lindbergh quickly became one of the greatest heroes America had ever known.

Lindbergh, however, was an intensely private man, and he grew to despise his fame. His private life had changed forever. People went to such great lengths to get a piece of him that they stole his dirty laundry for souvenirs! He wrote, "I've had enough fame for a dozen lives. It's not what it's cracked up to be."

Tragedy and controversy plagued Lindbergh after his flight. He was married in 1929. In 1932, his twenty-month-old son was kidnapped and later found murdered. An unemployed carpenter named Bruno Hauptmann was executed for the crime. Newspapers sensationalized the murder, calling it "the crime of the century." Reporters ignored the Lindberghs' grief and nagged the couple for interviews. Two photographers even broke into the Trenton, New Jersey, morgue and took pictures of the

murdered boy's body. The Lindberghs fled to Europe to seek peace.

In Europe, Lindbergh admired Nazi Germany's aviation industry. He also became an active member of a movement that hoped to keep the United States out of the new war that was brewing in Europe. He accepted a Medal of Honor presented to him by the head of the German Air Force, Hermann Goering. Critics charged that he was anti-American, anti-Jewish, and anti-British. Lindbergh denied all charges.

After World War II, Lindbergh finally faded from the public spotlight. He and his wife had five more children. He remained in the aviation industry and helped design aircraft. He was one of the designers of today's Boeing 747 jumbo

Charles Lindbergh in 1970, four years before his death

jet. In the 1960s, he spoke out for conservation of the nation's forests and against the killing of whales.

The *Spirit of St. Louis* now hangs in the National Air and Space Museum in Washington, D.C. The museum is part of the Smithsonian Institution. Before his death in 1974, Lindbergh often visited the Smithsonian to gaze at the aircraft he made famous. He would pull his hat over his eyes so he wouldn't be recognized.

Charles Lindbergh was far more than just a superb pilot. He was a curious mixture of mystic and mechanic, dreamer and engineer, technician and poet.

Above all, Lindbergh was a passionate believer in the wonders of science. But late in his life, he recognized that even science has its limits. He wrote, "It took me years to discover that science, with all its brilliance, lights only a middle chapter of creation. [It is] a chapter with both ends bordering on the infinite. One which can be forever expanded but never completed."

The Spirit of St. Louis *is now on display at the National Air and Space Museum along with many other landmarks in aviation history.*

INDEX

PHOTO CREDITS

Cover, Stock Montage, Inc.; 1, Lawrence D. Bell Collection/The Norman F. Sprague Memorial Library; 2, UPI/Minnesota Historical Society; 3, 4, UPI/Bettmann; 5, AP/Wide World; 6, Eastern National Park; 7 (top), Bettmann Archive; 7 (bottom), AP/Wide World; 8, UPI/Bettmann; 9, Brown Brothers; 10, Bettmann Archive; 11 (both photos), UPI/Bettmann; 12, AP/Wide World; 13, Minnesota Historical Society; 14 (bottom), UPI/Bettmann; 14 (top), 15 (top), 17, AP/Wide World; 15 (bottom), Courtesy United States Postal Service; 18, John M. Nobel/Minnesota Historical Society; 21, Bettmann Archive; 23, AP/Wide World; 24, Bettmann Archive; 25 (top), UPI/Bettmann; 25 (bottom), ©K. Dodge/New England Stock Photo; 26 (top, bottom left), Bettmann Archive; 26 (bottom right), Minnesota Historical Society; 26 (center photos), 27 (both photos), 28 (left), AP/Wide World; 28 (top), Stock Montage, Inc.; 29, 30, UPI/Bettmann; 31, ©Mikal Johansen/New England Stock Photo

Picture Identifications:
page 1: Thousands people swarm the *Spirit of St. Louis* as it lands in Paris.
page 2: Charles Lindbergh

Project Editors: Shari Joffe and Mark Friedman
Design and Electronic Composition: TJS Design
Photo Editor: Jan Izzo
Cornerstones of Freedom Logo: David Cunningham

ABOUT THE AUTHOR

R. Conrad Stein was born and grew up in Chicago. After serving in the U.S. Marine Corps, he attended the University of Illinois, where he earned a B.A. in history. He later studied in Mexico, where he received an advanced degree in fine arts.

Reading history is Mr. Stein's hobby. He tries to bring the excitement of history to his work. Mr. Stein has published many history books aimed at young readers. He lives in Chicago with his wife and their daughter Janna.